First Facts™

From Farm to Table

From Corn to Cereal

by Roberta Basel

Consultant:
Art Hill, Professor of Food Science
University of Guelph
Guelph, Ontario, Canada

Capstone
press
Mankato, Minnesota

First Facts is published by Capstone Press,
151 Good Counsel Drive, P.O. Box 669, Mankato, Minnesota 56002.
www.capstonepress.com

Library of Congress Cataloging-in-Publication Data
Basel, Roberta.
From corn to cereal / by Roberta Basel.
    p. cm.—(First facts. From farm to table)
    Includes bibliographical references (p. 23) and index.
    Summary: "An introduction to the basic concept of food production, distribution, and
consumption by tracing the production of cereal from corn to the finished product"—Provided
by publisher.
    ISBN 0-7368-4284-5 (hardcover)
    1. Cereals, Prepared—Juvenile literature. 2. Corn—Juvenile literature. I. Title. II. Series.
TP435.C4B37 2006
664'.756—dc22   2004029191

Editorial Credits
Jennifer Besel, editor; Jennifer Bergstrom, set designer; Ted Williams, book designer;
    Wanda Winch, photo researcher/photo editor

Photo Credits
Art Directors/Igor Bugandinov, 11; John Ellard, 16
Brand X Pictures/Bob Rashid, 7
Capstone Press/Karon Dubke, cover, 1, 5, 15, 19, 21
Corbis/Peter Yates, 17; Royalty-Free, 6, 9
David R. Frazier Photolibrary Inc., 10
Northern Crops Institute, Fargo, ND, USA, 14
Unicorn Stock Photos/Paula J. Harrington, 20
USDA/Larry Rana, 8
Wenger Manufacturing, Inc./Gerry Hertzel, 13

Table of Contents

Eating Cereal

Every day, people eat cereal with milk for breakfast. Some people eat dry cereal as a snack. Cereal can also be baked into cookies and other treats.

Cereal has to be made before it can be eaten. Making cereal takes many steps.

Fun Fact!
On average, each person in North America eats about 12 pounds (5 kilograms) of cereal every year.

Grain

Cereal is made from grain. A grain
is a small seed that can be eaten. One
kind of grain is corn. Some kinds of
cereal are made from corn.

Corn grows on corn plants. The corn plant is a large kind of grass. Its **stalk** can grow to almost 15 feet (4.5 meters) tall.

Growing Corn

Farmers plant corn seeds in spring. As the corn grows, **ears** form on the stalks. Under layers of **husk**, yellow **kernels** form on the ears.

In fall, the corn dries and turns
brown. Farmers use **combines** to
take the kernels off the corn plants.

Mills and Factories

Combines pour the corn kernels into large trailers. Trucks pull the full trailers from the fields to the **mills**.

Fun Fact!
Each ear of corn has about 800 kernels.

Mills use **machines** to **grind** the kernels into small pieces. These pieces are taken to **factories**. Factories make the corn pieces into cereal.

Cereal Flakes

At the factory, corn pieces, water, sugar, and other **ingredients** are mixed together. The mixture is cooked and broken into small clumps. These clumps are dried with hot air.

To make flakes, rollers press the clumps. Ovens then toast the flakes to make them golden and crispy.

Fun Fact!
Battle Creek, Michigan, is called the "cereal bowl of America." Most U.S. cereal is made there.

Other Shapes

Not all cereal is made into flakes. The cooked corn mixture can be put into another machine. This machine makes shapes, such as squares and circles.

The shapes are dried with hot air and put in another machine. This machine puffs up the shapes.

To the Store

Belts carry the flakes and shapes to another machine. This machine puts the cereal into plastic bags.

The bags are sealed and put
into boxes. Stores buy the cereal.
Airplanes, trucks, and trains carry
the cereal to the stores.

Where to Find Cereal

Cereal is sold almost everywhere food is sold. Grocery stores sell different kinds of cereal. Corn cereal comes in many shapes, sizes, colors, and flavors.

Fun Fact!
Cereal and soda are the two most commonly sold items at grocery stores.

Amazing but True!

Each year, corn is used to decorate the outside of a building in Mitchell, South Dakota. This building is the famous Corn Palace. The decorating starts in spring. Thousands of corn kernels are used to make pictures on the walls.

Hands On: Cereal Snack

You can make a tasty snack out of cornflakes cereal. Ask an adult to help you.

What You Need

¼ cup (60 mL) sugar
½ cup (120 mL) corn syrup
¼ cup (60 mL) margarine
6 cups (1.4 L) cornflakes cereal
1 cup (240 mL) peanuts

large saucepan
stirring spoon
cooking spray
cookie sheet
knife

What You Do

1. Put the sugar, corn syrup, and margarine in the saucepan.
2. Cook the mixture over medium heat. Bring the mixture to a boil. Let it boil for one minute, stirring constantly. Remove it from the heat.
3. Add the cereal and peanuts to the mixture in the saucepan. Stir everything together.
4. Coat the cookie sheet with the cooking spray.
5. Put the mixture on the cookie sheet. Spread it out so it is even. Let it cool.
6. Cut your snack into pieces. You can eat your snack by itself or with ice cream, pudding, or yogurt.
7. Keep leftovers in an airtight container in the refrigerator.

Glossary

combine (KOM-bine)—a farm machine used to harvest crops

ear (IHR)—the part of some plants on which grain or seeds grow

factory (FAK-tuh-ree)—a building where products are made in large amounts

grind (GRINDE)—to crush something into fine pieces

husk (HUHSK)—the outside covering of some seeds

ingredient (in-GREE-dee-uhnt)—an item used to make something else

kernel (KUR-nuhl)—the seed of a cereal plant

machine (muh-SHEEN)—a piece of equipment that is used to do a job

mill (MIL)—a place that grinds grain

stalk (STAWK)—the main stem of a plant

Read More

Hall, M. C. *Corn.* Food. Heinemann First Library. Chicago: Heinemann, 2003.

Hipp, Andrew. *Corn Inside and Out.* Getting into Nature. New York: PowerKids Press, 2004.

Mayo, Gretchen Will. *Cereal.* Where Does Our Food Come From? Milwaukee: Weekly Reader Early Learning Library, 2004.

Internet Sites

FactHound offers a safe, fun way to find Internet sites related to this book. All of the sites on FactHound have been researched by our staff.

Here's how:
1. Visit *www.facthound.com*
2. Type in this special code **0736842845** for age-appropriate sites. Or enter a search word related to this book for a more general search.
3. Click on the **Fetch It** button.

FactHound will fetch the best sites for you!

Index